WHAT THERAPY
MISSED,
YOUR SOUL
DEMANDS

A Spiritual guide to Trauma Healing
and True Forgiveness

MATIN AHAKI LAKEH

Disclaimer

The content presented in this book is based on the author's personal spiritual journey, research, and experiences. The techniques, practices, and teachings outlined within are shared for informational and educational purposes only and not intended as a substitute for the medical advice of physicians and psychologists. Results and outcomes from the application of these practices can vary greatly depending on the individual's level of faith, awareness, and spiritual maturity.

The author, publisher, and copyright holders expressly disclaim any and all responsibility, liability, or warranties regarding the success or failure of any practices outlined in this book, as well as the interpretation of its messages. The author makes no claims as to the effectiveness, accuracy, or suitability of any techniques or practices described.

By reading this book, the reader acknowledges and agrees that they take full responsibility for their own actions, practices, decisions, and interpretations in relation to the material contained herein.

The author, publisher, and copyright holders shall not be held liable for any claims, damages, or legal issues arising from the use or misuse of the information, practices, or ideas presented in this book.

Contents

PART ONE

Introduction to the Soul's Healing Journey

Preface

In this fast-moving world filled with emotional noise, spiritual confusion, and constant pressure, many of us silently carry the weight of mental and emotional overwhelm. This burden often stems from unresolved past experiences such as old wounds, broken relationships, unhealed trauma, and deep spiritual disconnection. These experiences quietly shape our present lives, influencing our decisions and overall well-being, while leaving lasting internal scars on the soul. There is an urgent need for intentional healing, emotional support, and spiritual restoration to help us reconnect with ourselves and move forward with clarity, peace, and purpose.

What Therapy Missed, Your Soul Demands is both a reflection of my personal healing journey and a guidebook to share the insights I've gained over the years as a spiritual practitioner. This book is for those who are ready to release what no longer serves them, forgive, and reconnect with their true self. I've walked this path—through emotional trauma, spiritual emptiness, and the search for lasting peace—and I understand how difficult it is to move forward when past pain still lingers beneath the surface. This book is written for that very purpose: to help guide you toward soul healing, awareness, and inner alignment.

Along my journey, I discovered a powerful truth: real healing doesn't happen without spiritual understanding. Therapy can offer insight, tools, and emotional awareness. However, it often stops short in providing what the soul truly needs, causing many to feel stuck. They gain insight but not release, language but not liberation. What therapy sometimes misses is the soul's demand: to be seen, to be understood in the context of spiritual growth, and to heal within the deeper architecture of divine truth. Without alignment to spiritual guidelines like soul wisdom, divine timing, Law of Cause and Effect, and other universal principals, the healing process can feel like a loop—insight without closure, effort without peace. To heal trauma and forgive meaningfully, you must first understand the deeper reasons behind the events in your lives. You must see them not just as misfortune and suffering, but as part of a greater spiritual curriculum which will be covered in this book.

Everyone tells you to "forgive and forget," but no one tells you *how*—or, more importantly, *why*. This book changes that. It offers more than insight and techniques. It offers clarity. It explains the spiritual laws and metaphysical principles that govern our lives, while also providing enlightenment on how they work, so that you can experience *real* forgiveness and *true* emotional release. Ultimately, this book is for those who are ready to stop the endless cycle of rehashing the past and instead step into a new way of being—one rooted in purpose, truth, and freedom.

This is not just another self-help book. It's a practical, spiritual guide—concise, intentional, and transformational. Through the insights and practices within this book, you will initiate a more profound comprehension of your inner world than you have ever previously accessed. You will become your own therapist—not by earning a certificate but by awakening the wisdom already within you. With spiritual understanding as your foundation, you'll no longer need to revisit the same pain repeatedly. Instead, you'll gain the tools you need to release it, transcend it, and finally live with clarity, purpose, and peace.

In writing this book, I've kept one priority at the center: delivering authentic, transformational value while still respecting your time. I've remained deeply mindful of the modern reader's reality—limited time, mental overwhelm, and a craving for depth over fluff. Too often, people invest in books—even bestsellers—only to find them padded with repetition or surface-level advice. This book is different. It is concise, actionable, and powerful and full of enriching chapters crafted with clear intention.

Whether you are just beginning your spiritual journey or seeking to deepen it, this book will meet you where you are. It is for those who are ready to confront their past with compassion, take radical responsibility for their healing, understand the why behind their pain, and let go—for real this time. If you're looking for practical wisdom rooted in authenticity and spiritual truth and the transformative power of true forgiveness, then you'll find it here.

Thank you for allowing me to be part of your healing journey. May this book serve as a light on your path, a reflection of your true self, and a reminder that healing is not only possible but inevitable when you walk in alignment with who you truly are.

Introduction

Before beginning any spiritual practice, it is essential to first release the emotional burdens of the past: painful memories, unresolved trauma, and the constant noise of overthinking. Only after this release can the energy centers of the body fully open to receive the flow of life force that sustains and guides us.

Look around you. How many people do you know who seem to have everything yet still struggle with anxiety, depression, or a deep sense of emptiness? Despite financial stability or outward success, many silently suffer from mental and emotional challenges that money and materials alone cannot fix. This is because true healing, happiness, and life satisfaction do not necessarily come from external achievements and material wealth but from within—through clarity of mind, peace, and alignment with our higher selves. Even powerful universal laws like the Law of Attraction and the Law of Vibration only work in your favor when your inner foundation is clear and balanced. If the soul is burdened and the energy field is chaotic, then what you attract will reflect that disorder, not your desires.

A damaged soul cannot think clearly, and a tired mind cannot make wise decisions. When the heart is burdened and the mind is overwhelmed, it becomes nearly impossible to connect with your higher self or access deep wisdom from within. This inner imbalance eventually affects the physical body, leading to mental and physical health issues. No matter what you achieve or gain, true happiness will remain out of reach when the soul is unsettled and the mind is at war with itself.

Trauma, in its essence, is not the event or wound itself but rather the consequence of suppressed emotional energy when healing is needed the most. True spiritual growth begins when the past no longer dictates the present—when the wounds no longer speak louder than our purpose.

This book is a foundational step on your path to healing and energetic restoration. It is especially intended for those who have low self-esteem due to experiencing emotional pain, relationship wounds, or spiritual disconnection as a child or an adult. You will be guided through effective techniques for trauma healing, forgiveness, and energy cleansing that will allow your inner healing to unfold naturally.

One of the deepest sources of human suffering is the belief that the world is unjust—that those who harm others thrive, while good-hearted people suffer. But through the spiritual insights in this book, you will come to understand that the universe operates according to profound laws of balance and divine justice, many of which are often invisible to the human eye. This understanding marks the beginning of true inner peace.

As you familiarize yourself with these universal principles and apply the techniques in this book, you'll begin to dissolve the weight of past trauma, sharpen your ability to self-reflect during challenging moments, and experience the freedom that comes with real forgiveness—of others and of yourself. You will also raise your energetic vibration, unlocking the door to conscious manifestation and intuitive living. *Because true healing doesn't begin in a clinic; it begins with consciousness.* The moment you become self-aware is the moment you begin to heal. Half the cure is in recognizing the truth within you. The rest flows from there.

In the early chapters, you will learn foundational spiritual concepts, including karma, reincarnation, soul mission,

and testing and training, as well as the principles surrounding them. As you progress into the later chapters, you'll learn
practical healing techniques such as Libra, Etheric Cord
Cutting, and the Full Moon Forgiveness Ritual. These will
empower you to clear emotional blockages, release karmic
ties, and achieve lasting transformation, and you can return
to them again and again whenever needed during your journey to reach inner freedom and peace.

Nothing is more important than happiness in life. After
reading this book, you will come to see how you imposed
unnecessary grief, shame, anger, and fear—even envy, com-
petition, and conflict—upon yourself. You will realize how
much of your energy was drained by unnecessary distractions that prevented you from reaching the higher purpose
you are here to fulfill.

My deepest intention for this book is to help you find
your way to authentic happiness, emotional clarity, and a
profound sense of inner contentment by finally answering
the question, "Why me?" May you come to know yourself
as the creator of your life, fully responsible for your happiness, regardless of external circumstances and the actions of
others. Peace, abundance, health, and fulfillment are already
within you. This is a journey of remembering.

How to Use This Book

Whether you are just starting your spiritual journey or already familiar with some metaphysical principles, I encourage you to approach this book with an open heart and mind. Set aside any preconceived notions and allow yourself to discover the simplicity and depth of the teachings within.

To fully benefit, I recommend reading this book in a quiet, peaceful setting—free from distraction. I urge you not to skip any part of it, including the preface, introduction, and glossary. Each section offers something valuable, and the entire book is like a puzzle—each piece complements the others, and nothing should be missed. Take your time and avoid haste. During your first read, simply absorb the concepts and familiarize yourself with the material. Then, during your second pass, begin to apply the techniques covered slowly and mindfully. With consistent practice, you may begin to notice real emotional and energetic shifts within one to two weeks.

The techniques in the latter chapters of this book rely on the use of meditation and spiritual visualization. For best results, it's important to begin with a cleansed energy field and environment. Please consider the following preparations:

✓ **Take a hot bath before your practice.** This helps cleanse physical impurities and energetically prepares the body through relaxation and purification.

✓ **Wear light, comfortable clothing.** Avoid tight or restrictive garments. If possible, choose white clothing that loosely covers the body, including undergarments, to create a sense of energetic openness and neutrality. Wearing black garments during practice is not recommended.

✓ **Cleanse your space.** Before meditating, lightly spray your meditation space with a natural mixture of vinegar, sea salt, and water. This helps release negative energy and create a purified setting for your practice. You can also light incense for environmental cleansing as well.

✓ **Improve your meditation experience.** Light a candle and inhale the scent of fresh flowers or rose water while playing soft sounds like nature melodies, spa music, or any meditation tracks in 432 Hz to create a peaceful atmosphere. Apply a small amount of rose water between your eyebrows and over your throat and heart center to stimulate clarity in your major chakras.

Note: *This book assumes a foundational understanding of meditation and spiritual energy work. While I will not attempt to convince you of the existence or effectiveness of spiritual practices, I will guide you through the direct experience of them. Your own results will be your greatest proof.*

PART TWO

Opening the Heart to Healing

Awakening the Soul to True Healing

Before we begin practical techniques, it's important to establish a foundational understanding of key spiritual concepts which will guide and support your healing process. These principles—karma, reincarnation, and soul contracts—are essential to making sense of your emotional experiences on a deeper level. They offer a new lens through which you can view your pain, relationships, and life purpose. Karma helps us understand repeated challenging patterns; soul contracts shed light on difficult relationships; and reincarnation gives perspective to true life purpose.

You do not need to adopt any specific belief system, but staying open to these ideas will help you fully engage in the healing process. Just as you wouldn't begin advanced mathematics without first understanding basic arithmetic, the same principle applies here. The methods in this book will be most effective once you're familiar with the spiritual truths that form their foundation.

When you are physically wounded, you treat the injury by disinfecting the wound, applying ointment, putting on a bandage, and possibly using laser treatment to remove the scar. Your soul requires that same level of attention and healing—especially for deep scars and pains of the past. Your soul needs nourishment just as much as your body does. The techniques in this book are designed to help you release emotional burdens and pave the way for true happiness and spiritual ascension. Healing is not about temporary fixes. It's about deep, lasting transformation. As you revisit old memories and past events, emotions like anger, regret, jealousy, and resentment can resurface. Without letting go of the past and practicing forgiveness, you will never attain the stability or sustainable results you desire from spiritual methods or practices.

In the following sections, we'll explore these essential concepts to prepare your heart, mind, and energy field for the transformative techniques ahead.

Why Emotional Pain Still Lingers

Have you ever wondered why, despite your best efforts, you keep getting pulled back into emotional pain or memories you'd rather forget? To grow personally, socially, financially, and—most importantly—spiritually, you must learn to stay present and look ahead. Yet, even still, so many people remain stuck in the past, reliving the same emotions, despite any earthly practices they try. The question is: why do earthly techniques only offer temporary relief?

Many people unknowingly remain trapped in the past, carrying the weight of emotional wounds, unresolved trauma, and painful experiences. These invisible burdens often follow them everywhere, even into moments of joy or success, quietly preventing real peace. As a result, even those who appear to "have it all"—supportive relationships, financial comfort, and good health—may still feel unsettled inside are thus unable to access lasting happiness.

While these struggles might seem small to others, or even dismissed as exaggerations, the truth is much deeper. From a spiritual and metaphysical perspective, many people are old souls with well-developed spiritual memories that go unrecognized but remain deeply active. Their heightened sensitivity to negative words, low vibrational energy, and unresolved emotions is not weakness but a sign of soul maturity which, in many cases, they are not aware of.

Some seek healing through therapy, books, or podcasts, yet they continue to feel that something is missing. Others carry lingering grief, regret, or anger from past experiences—whether from family dynamics, childhood wounds, or relationships of any kind. Often, they struggle to fully express or even identify their pain, especially when life calls for emotional clarity, presence, or connection. This is because spiritual and energetic wounds often exist beneath conscious awareness—beyond what the mind alone can access or heal.

Before exploring any techniques, you must first learn the foundational spiritual concepts—because true healing can only begin when you understand what you're healing from.

Why We Stay Emotionally Tied to the Past

Have you ever felt emotionally attached to someone long after they've left your life—perhaps even years after contact has ended? This could be a friend, romantic partner, family member, or even colleague. That lingering emotional bond is not just in your head. It's energetic.

Whenever you form a meaningful connection with another person, an invisible energy cord called Etheric Cord is created. These cords link our energy fields and remain intact regardless of physical distance or time. The more intense the relationship—whether loving or painful—the stronger the cord.

This explains why certain people continue to affect you emotionally, mentally, and even physically long after the relationship has ended. A part of your soul remains entangled in these unresolved energetic threads, quietly draining your vitality, influencing your choices, and keeping you emotionally stuck.

To truly heal and regain your spiritual clarity, you must first understand this deeper truth: You are not a physical being who has a soul. You are a soul, temporarily expressing itself in physical form.

And because of that, healing cannot rely on earthly methods alone. While therapy, journaling, or talking things through can be helpful, they are often not enough. Real release, real freedom requires spiritual techniques, including meditation of energy cord cutting techniques, which you'll learn in a later chapter.

Let's begin by understanding how these cords are formed and how to identify them, then, we will discuss how to gently yet powerfully cut the ones which no longer serve your soul's journey.

Why Spiritual
Practices Matter

Before we go any further, let me be clear: the insights in this book are not meant to discredit science or any profession. On the contrary, I hold deep respect for all individuals who devote their lives to helping others—especially psychologists, doctors, and therapists.

However, despite their valuable work, there remains a missing link in most modern healing systems: spirituality. This absent dimension is often the reason why therapy or medication, though helpful in the short term, may not offer lasting transformation in many cases. Most medical or psychological approaches are designed to treat symptoms, not root causes. But physical and mental illnesses that aren't traced back to their energetic or spiritual origin are like pesky weeds that can regrow anytime, without any water or sunlight.

Let's bring this closer to your lived experience. Have you ever had an argument then suddenly developed a headache? Faced a stressful situation and lost sleep? Walked into a gathering and instantly felt tense, then reached for antacids to soothe the discomfort? These reactions aren't random. They're the result of energetic disturbances within and around you that can be fixed with modern medical and psychological techniques. But what about the deep underlying energetic causes that need to be addressed?

When your psyche—the bridge between body and soul—is overwhelmed or damaged, it doesn't just cause emotional distress; it weakens your immune system, affects your organs, and blocks spiritual clarity. When left unaddressed, this disconnection can lead to chronic illness, emotional imbalance, and persistent dissatisfaction with life— even if everything "seems fine" externally.

That's why healing at the soul level is essential. Medications and sedatives may soothe pain temporarily, but they rarely address the spiritual scars underneath to prevent them from coming back. True healing begins when we stop treating symptoms and start listening to the soul.

PART THREE

Understanding the Soul's Purpose

Why the Soul Reincarnates

Reincarnation is the concept that a soul or spirit is reborn into a new body after the death of its previous one. This cycle of birth, death, and rebirth continues until the soul reaches a state of spiritual liberation, enlightenment, or completion. What's important to understand is that reincarnation is never mandatory. It is based on the soul's free will in alignment with universe principles. This means that a soul chooses—of its own accord—to return to Earth in a new body to fulfill a higher purpose, continue its learning, or assist others. It is always a conscious decision, not a punishment or obligation.

Karma and reincarnation are interwoven truths that

complete one another and are often spoken of together. In this book, we will not delve deeply into the intricate details of karma and reincarnation, but it's important to briefly touch on their significance in order to understand the deeper workings of life.

Some events in our lives, though they may seem unjust or unfair, are part of a larger cosmic justice. Often, the struggles we face in this life are the result of unresolved past-life experiences that must be reconciled. Oftentimes, one human lifetime is not long enough to fully experience the effects of their positive and negative karma, so this energy carries over into future lives.

This is the essence of universal justice. You might have wondered why certain individuals pass away peacefully while others suffer for an extended period of time. But rest assured: justice is an ever-present force that operates beyond the physical plane of human understanding. Our limited perspective often leads to misunderstandings of this cosmic truth. The path to spiritual growth may not always be smooth, but even still, understanding it is essential to discovering the deeper purpose of our existence.

Human beings are infinite souls who choose to manifest in physical form as an act of free will. Most souls have lived hundreds—or even thousands—of lifetimes on Earth, each in different regions, cultures, genders, and life circumstances. While the physical world often feels more real, it is the spiritual realm that holds the greater truth. Soul evolution is guaranteed in the spiritual realm, but wisdom growth in the spiritual realm occurs at a much slower pace than it does here on Earth. That is why souls voluntarily choose to incarnate: Earth offers an accelerated path for learning, growing, and transformation. However, it's important to remember that not all souls automatically ascend by merely coming to Earth, as life on Earth carries its own risks and challenges that can lead to spiritual fall. Some may descend if they become entangled in illusion, distraction, or negativity. The material world, often influenced by ego, temptation, and other dark forces, can pull souls away from their true path if they are not spiritually grounded. Earth is a place of great testing and great potential.

The purpose of reincarnation is often one of the following:

- To protect or support loved ones affected by past-life actions
- To resolve unfinished karma
- To fulfill a soul mission
- To undergo necessary tests and spiritual training in order to speed up soul Ascension

In each case, reincarnation is a conscious choice made

by your soul—also known as your Higher Self—even if you don't consciously remember making that choice in this lifetime. That's why it's important to understand that life, no matter how difficult it may seem at times, is a divine gift. Every experience serves a higher purpose.

You are here for a reason. So, embrace your life, make the most of it, and don't waste a single day.

Understanding Karma

While the word "karma" is widely used in conversations, it is often misunderstood or misrepresented. Many associate karma with punishment or negativity, yet at its core, karma is neutral. It simply reflects the universal principle of cause and effect: you receive what you give. If your actions, words, and intentions are positive, then those energies will return to you. If they're harmful, then that energy will also come back to you in some form.

What truly shapes karma isn't just what you do or say but the intention behind your actions, thoughts, and words. The intention is the seed of karma. While some experience the results of their karma during their current lifetime, others may carry it into future lifetimes. Every choice you make contributes to the energetic pattern your soul is weaving. In

this way, karma is not punishment or fate; it's about conscious responsibility and soul evolution. Karma is the echo
of actions, returning to us in ways we may not expect but
always in perfect balance.

People often overlook self-reflection, spiritual connection, and accountability during times of comfort and ease.
It's usually during moments of pain, hardship, or loss that
they become more open to the divine and more willing to
examine their inner world. Karma can manifest in many
forms—challenging work situations, recurring relationship
patterns, delays in progress, illness, or financial setbacks—
each carrying a lesson and an opportunity for growth,
awareness, and realignment with a higher path.

When someone is caught in a karmic cycle—whether they realize it or not—approaching the experience with
compassion and self-awareness allows for transformation.
By recognizing the deeper lesson and understanding what
must be learned or released, they can break free from the
pattern. Otherwise, they may remain stuck in a karmic loop,
repeating the same challenges until they awaken to the way
forward.

This is why daily meditation is essential for healing. It
helps cultivate a deeper connection to your subconscious
mind, the universe, or divine intelligence. Through stillness

and presence, we gain the clarity to see where healing is needed and where we must grow. Without this connection, life's
challenges can feel overwhelming and directionless. But
with it, we align ourselves with wisdom, peace, and purpose.

Sometimes, the hardships you face are simply the result
of someone else's choices impacting your life through the
universal Law of Cause and Effect—not necessarily your
karma. It's important to pause, reflect, and look inward to
discern whether what you're experiencing is part of a greater life justice at work. If you sense that it is, then taking
thoughtful and appropriate action becomes essential. This
process begins with deep self-reflection, sincere learning,
and heartfelt gratitude for the opportunity to recognize and
address the situation. True remorse, paired with committed
steps toward correction, completes the path to resolution.

What's important to understand is that we are not
all-knowing souls sitting in judgment whenever hardship
strikes us or others. Many mistakenly believe that every difficulty is simply "karma." However, karma is just one of the
four core reasons for a soul's reincarnation. Therefore, we
should never judge others or assume their struggles are solely
due to karma. We are not equipped to fully understand people's true intentions or their greater life plan.

Testing and Training

Some challenges we face are not the result of past actions (karma) but rather spiritual tests—divinely chosen opportunities for growth. For example, someone might be offered a great deal of money in exchange for something unethical, testing their integrity. Another may experience a sudden accident or misfortune that shakes their faith in the divine. Or someone might face a dangerous situation—like encountering a wild animal during a peaceful walk—not as punishment, but as a chance to face fear and awaken inner courage. Someone might feel broken at times, but it's in those moments that they are presented with the opportunity to discover their inner strength and intelligence, boosting their confidence and allowing them to realize that they are capable of overcoming anything.

Do not forget that we live in a world governed by the Law of Cause and Effect. The actions, decisions, and energy of others can absolutely impact us. Not every misfortune is necessarily karmic, but it is still meaningful. So be mindful. When you face hardship, pause and reflect—not in self-blame but with curiosity. Ask yourself: What is this trying to teach me? How do my thoughts, emotions, or unresolved energy play a role? The answer resides within you and may lead you to clarity—not condemnation—which is where healing begins.

Many people act as if they are divine judges, assuming that when something harmful happens to someone, it must be because they are a "bad soul," and when something good happens, it means they are lucky or spiritually superior. But there is far more to these experiences than the limited physical mind can understand. The divine plan operates on levels beyond our immediate perception. What appears as misfortune or blessing may be part of a soul's sacred agreement, spiritual lesson, or karmic resolution—not necessarily reflection of one's worth or goodness.

Likewise, someone's material wealth or success is not proof of their spiritual virtue or divine favor. Money and comfort do not mean a person is spiritually superior, just as pain, illness, or poverty do not mean someone is a bad soul. Every soul walks a unique path, designed with sacred purpose and specific lessons.

Therefore, you never truly know the soul behind the face. Someone who appears happy, wealthy, or powerful today may have endured unimaginable suffering in a previous life. And as for you, you don't fully remember your own past lifetimes either. That's why comparing your journey to someone else's is not only unfair but also spiritually short-sighted. This life could be your tenth reincarnation, while the person you're watching might be on their hundredth. Each soul evolves at its own pace, with its own lessons, timelines, and karmic paths. What you see now is just one frame in a much longer spiritual film. Instead of comparison, choose compassion—for yourself and for others. Trust that where you are right now is exactly where your soul needs to be for its next step in growth.

In conclusion, the challenges we face in life are not always the result of past karma; they can also be spiritual tests designed for our growth. These divine opportunities push us to confront our fears, strengthen our character, and deepen our connection with the divine. Rather than viewing hardships as punishment, we must approach them with curiosity and compassion, recognizing them as essential lessons on our soul's journey. By embracing these experiences, we unlock our inner potential and align ourselves with the divine plan, trusting that each challenge is guiding us toward our higher purpose.

Soul Agreement

The human soul is an infinite being that continues to live in the spiritual realm after physical death. In that realm, life goes on beyond the body, and souls continue to grow, evolve, and fulfill higher purposes. Souls with similar levels of wisdom are often grouped together for higher purposes—such as receiving spiritual training and helping guide or support other souls who are at earlier stages of their evolution.

Sometimes, souls from the same spiritual level and soul group make agreements before incarnating on Earth to play specific roles in each other's lives. They may appear as parents, siblings, cousins, friends, or even as challenging figures. Nonetheless, each role serves a purpose in the soul's growth and karmic journey. These roles may offer support, make amends, or create challenges that help resolve unfinished dynamics from past lives. Such encounters serve as opportunities for spiritual growth, healing, and karmic balance. That's why you sometimes meet people and instantly feel like you already knew them—even without any prior connection in this life. These individuals are likely souls you've shared a deep bond with—either from being on the same spiritual level in the spirit world or from playing significant roles in each other's lives in a previous incarnation.

It's not always easy to understand the purpose behind a particular situation or person's presence in your life—whether it's a divine test, karmic lesson, soul agreement, or part of your soul mission. Soul mission carries depth beyond the scope of this book, so it won't be covered. However, with consistent daily meditation and sincere requests for divine guidance, you will begin to receive answers. These may come through signs, intuition, dreams, or other subtle forms.

That being said, what's most important to remember is this: face difficulties with a smile and an open heart and genuinely ask yourself, "What am I going to learn this time?" Now that you understand your challenges fall into one of the four high-purpose categories, you can embrace them as tools for spiritual growth and wisdom. As you learn the intended lesson, the situation will often begin to dissolve or transform naturally. If not, it may return in different forms until the lesson is fully integrated.

Now that you've begun to understand the deeper truth about karma, reincarnation, and the soul's journey, you may start to see life through a more compassionate and empowered lens. Life is a gift, and hardships are not punishments but invitations to rise in soul level. And every person you encounter, even those who hurt or challenge you, serves as a teacher for your evolution.

Even if you were born into a region, culture, or family that feels misaligned with your soul—or even caused you harm—know this: at the soul level, you chose them. Before incarnating, your spirit was shown a range of life scenarios, and you consciously selected the one that would best serve your soul's growth—even if you can't remember it now.

Reincarnation is a natural part of the soul's journey—a path of learning and growth, not a form of punishment. It is a sacred opportunity to evolve, to heal, and to complete the work your soul began long ago.

What Role Does Free Will Play in Your Healing

Having free will means you are in control of your mind, body, and spirit, and that you are fully responsible for your actions. The awareness of this responsibility empowers you to face any challenge with resilience—even with a smile—because you know that every choice you make either nourishes your soul or weakens it. The universe constantly sends you signs in many forms: through people's words, a picture, a poem, song lyrics, a fleeting thought, or even a sudden shift in feeling. Learning to recognize these signs and distinguish them takes time and effort, but with practice, it becomes easier. Trusting your intuition over time will become a nature, although it requires great patience and awareness to discern in the beginning.

It's also important to note that life events occur for a variety of reasons. Some happen accidentally, while others arise from intentional actions—such as violence or betrayal—which are the result of misused free will, and not part of the divine plan. Yet, many events in our lives are karmic in nature, and before returning to Earth, souls often make agreements with others to undergo certain challenges. Sometimes, these challenges involve experiencing the pain they once caused in order to accelerate their spiritual growth. This is because spiritual growth progresses at a much slower rate in the spiritual realm than on Earth.

On the other hand, many events are the result of your own choices, as free will is an essential part of life's journey. Even reincarnation is not forced upon you; it is a decision your soul makes to continue its evolution and mission. Viewing your life through a spiritual lens—accepting its ups and downs as part of a divine plan—shifts your perception. Life is not a burden but a sacred opportunity, a divine gift for transformation.

Whenever you feel the urge to judge someone harshly for their actions, pause and ask yourself: "I have lived this life many times over. Perhaps in this life, my soul is more mature, but was I successful in my past lives? Did I cause harm in other lives?"

Those who achieve perfection in their life and fulfill their earthly mission will not need to return to Earth. So, if you are still here, it means you have countless untraveled paths and unexperienced lessons to be learned. If forgiveness is not granted in this lifetime, then those same souls may reappear in future incarnations for karmic resolution. The choice is yours: to forgive and release or to hold onto resentment. You must understand that there is no guarantee you will act differently in the next life, and the cycle of karma may continue.

PART FOUR

Practical Soul Healing Techniques

Trauma Healing and Forgiveness Techniques

N ow that you have a fundamental understanding of the soul's journey, universal laws, the spiritual realm, and the invisible forces that govern it, you are ready to dive into the core techniques of soul healing and forgiveness. These tools will free you from anything holding you back from progression.

In this section, you'll be guided through three powerful and transformative techniques—Libra, Etheric Cord Cutting, and the Full Moon Forgiveness Ritual—each carefully designed to help you release painful memories, shift destructive thought patterns, and detach from energetic ties to those who have hurt you. Unlike conventional approaches, these methods integrate psychological insight with spiritual wisdom to facilitate lasting emotional and energetic healing. When practiced in sequence, they allow for true release and personal renewal. By incorporating these practices, you will develop the ability to self-analyze with fairness and clarity in challenging situations, release negative attachments, and embrace forgiveness wholeheartedly.

This time is different from all the times before. You have the power to permanently release the burdens that have weighed on your soul and caused physical discomfort. This is your time for spiritual healing, transformation, and ascension.

I wish each of you a path of healing, spiritual growth, and profound transformation. May this book illuminate your path to peace, happiness, and inner freedom.

1. Libra Technique

The Libra Technique is a method of deep self-reflection and analysis that uncovers the hidden roots of emotional trauma. This process helps bring suppressed emotions to the surface, offering space for expression and understanding. It also addresses lingering guilt, shame, or self-blame that may be obstructing your healing.

Through honest introspection, guided writing exercises, and the integration of karmic principles, you will begin to clear mental clutter and prevent emotional patterns from resurfacing. This technique not only facilitates mental clarity but also reinforces your sense of inner justice, helping you make peace with your past through understanding rather than judgment.

2. Etheric Cord Cutting Ritual

The Etheric Cord Cutting technique is a spiritual practice rooted in visualization and energy healing. Influenced by the principles of hypnotherapy, it helps you identify and sever the invisible energetic attachments—known as etheric cords—that form during emotionally charged relationships or traumatic encounters.

Once the Libra Technique has helped you process and understand the psychological roots of these connections, etheric cord cutting allows you to release lingering energetic influence, ensuring that emotional pain and toxic patterns are not carried forward into future relationships or experiences.

3. Full Moon Forgiveness Ritual

The final technique in this process is a ritual focused on true forgiveness, liberation, and permanent release. This technique is performed during the powerful phase of the full Moon. This ritual supports the dissolution of negative karmic ties and facilitates the cultivation of positive energy and intention which helps you with true forgiveness.

By aligning your healing work with the Moon's natural cycle, this practice not only stabilizes the breakthroughs achieved through the first two techniques but also sets the stage for powerful manifestation work during the new Moon.

Let's dive deeper into each of these techniques.

Libra Technique

The Libra Technique is the foundational method for healing the soul and releasing trauma through honest self-analysis and emotional awareness. Rooted in the principles of balance, justice, and deep inner reflection, this technique guides you through a structured process to free yourself from the emotional burdens of the past. When learned and applied properly, it not only helps release past traumas but also ensures that future challenging situations do not turn into trauma.

This method consists of five transformative stages, each encouraging honesty, compassion, and spiritual insight. To engage fully in this process, you'll need a pen and notebook, a quiet space, and a willingness to meet yourself where you are—with courage and kindness.

Forgiveness brings freedom and lightness. When you truly experience this freedom, you begin to think more clearly, make better decisions, regain your self-confidence, and break free from the exhausting cycle of self-blame. The Libra Technique helps you reach this state by transforming the way you perceive your past. Through this process, you'll learn to view every situation from the perspective of experience—no matter how painful—not as something to be erased, but as a chapter in your evolution.

You are not meant to forget past events, as doing so may leave you vulnerable to experiencing this pain again and potentially being trapped in the same cycle of suffering. The true purpose of this technique is not to erase memories but to release the emotional charge attached to them by fully acknowledging and releasing suppressed emotions. The goal is to make the painful memories less intense, accept your experiences, and grow from them.

This technique is one of the most effective methods and can be powerful on its own. Trust the process, and when the time is right, apply it step by step with honesty and patience. For optimal results and enhanced effectiveness, it is recommended to perform this technique during the new Moon phase within the first seven days, as long as the Moon is not in the Scorpio Zodiac sign.

The Five Stages of the Libra Technique
1. Review the Memories and Write Them Down

Find a quiet and peaceful place where you can be alone and undisturbed. After your daily meditation, revisit any painful memories that still haunt you—those experiences you've been unable to let go of. Write them down in a notebook, capturing as many details as possible to help release the emotional weight. Approach this exercise as if you were explaining the event to a divine being or a wise, impartial judge and offer a thorough and honest account. During this process, you may feel distress, and emotions like anger or sadness may resurface, leading to temporary discomfort. Know that this emotional upheaval is natural, but trust that it will not last forever. The act of confronting and expressing these emotions is the first step to healing.

2. Rate the Memories

Rate each painful memory on a scale of one to ten. This step is crucial and must be done with complete honesty. For instance, if the death of a loved one would score a 10/10 on your mental scale, an illness might be a 9, and betrayal an 8. That being said, disrespect or an argument shouldn't be rated as 8. While it's very possible that this disagreement has been given a 9 in your mind for many years, now is the time to review everything critically. Take a moment to assess whether the intensity you previously assigned to these events was justified. You may have exaggerated the impact over time. Write down both the score you initially gave at the time of the event and the one you feel is more accurate now, then compare them. Reflect on whether you've mourned it excessively and then allow yourself to grieve the event according to its true emotional weight and nothing more.

3. Evaluate Your Role

At this stage, it is important to reflect on your own role in the situation. While you cannot control external factors such as society, fate, or the choices of others, you can examine your own actions. Ask yourself: is the other person always to blame? Personally, I believe that even when someone appears to have harmed an innocent person, whether physically or emotionally—the one who was hurt may also bear some responsibility as well. This is because he could have defended himself, chosen a different course of action, or at least established a stronger boundary from the beginning. Of course, there are exceptions to this, however.

That being said, in every situation, it's essential to identify your own contribution, no matter how small it may seem, either through your choices, responses, or lack of action. Whether your share in the situation is one percent or eighty percent, the key is to approach it with fairness and honesty. By conducting a fair self-analysis, you gain a clearer perspective and allow yourself to judge the situation more fairly with an open mind and heart.

If you examine past events closely, especially instances where you were hurt by people close to you such as betrayal, theft, or deceit, you may realize that in most cases, you had a sense something was wrong. Your intuition, coming from your subconscious mind, likely warned you through feelings or subtle signs, but you may have chosen to ignore them. It's important to acknowledge even the smallest part you may have played in these situations. The goal here is not self-blame but learning from your mistakes. If you don't learn from mistakes, you will be doomed to repeat the same patterns in this life and future lives until you do learn because of the universe karmic law and the principle it is governed with.

In rare cases where you find no clear personal responsibility whatsoever, understand that the situation may stem from unresolved karma—either from this life or a past one—divine testing, and spiritual training, or the effects of other people's choices. In either case, sincerely ask the divine and your spirit guides for forgiveness, both for the present situation and any unresolved karma carried over from past lives. Ask genuinely for help, guidance, and clear signs. Remember, it is not the difficulty of the experience that clears the karma but the understanding and the lessons you take from it.

4. List the Gains

Now, take a moment to reflect on what you have gained from your pains and traumas. Was it just suffering, or did it also offer you something valuable at the end? Many of the most successful people in the world achieved success after enduring heartbreak, loneliness, pain, failure, or other difficult experiences. Even during the most challenging times, there is often a glimmer of light waiting to be found. Seek it and uncover it.

For example, someone who has experienced assault may

choose to become a counselor, helping people who feel overlooked. A person who has gone bankrupt may publish a book sharing valuable experiences to save others from financial ruin. A person who was raised in a broken home or around addiction may make more conscious choices in marriage and parenting. Are these experiences without value?

Seek that glimmer of light within the pain because this path will lead you to your true destination. Write down the positives aspects of these difficult events, read them aloud, repeat them, and learn from them. It's possible that from those very hardships, you might find your life's true purpose.

5. Ask for Forgiveness and Express Gratitude

Ask for forgiveness for the probable karmic imprints of your current and past lives that have brought you to this point, aligning with the justice of the universe. Seek forgiveness from your guiding spirit and your guardian angels, who constantly offer guidance via your heart and intuition, even though due to material distractions, mental fog, or lack of belief you may not have listened to their warnings. It's best to perform this step both aloud and in writing to reinforce its impact.

Throughout the process, allow yourself to grieve as much as necessary. Remember, recalling painful memories is not more difficult than experiencing them. The fact that you have the courage to confront these emotions and participate in the healing process is truly courageous, as many people try to avoid facing the truth. An important aspect of grieving is discipline. Yes, you read that correctly—discipline! Set a clear boundary for yourself, such as allowing half an hour for crying or dedicating three hours for solitude each day until you feel relief for a maximum period of a week. Do not extend beyond that time. While it's important to give yourself the time you need, you'll be amazed at how quickly you will encounter a renewed, motivated, and stronger version of yourself by setting a mourning period.

During this process, it is highly recommended to engage in practices such as reading relevant books, meditating, communicating with the divine from the heart, confiding in a wise and trustworthy friend, seeking guidance from a skilled counselor, maintaining healthy social connections, adopting a lifestyle change, and practicing yoga if needed. The type of issues you are dealing with, the length of time you've carried them, your environment, spiritual level, and personal characteristics—all play significant roles in the degree of emotional harm.

Sometimes, the first step in healing your soul is simply having someone listen to you, helping to bring those buried emotions to the surface. As mentioned before, the wound is not trauma itself but the consequence of not expressing the emotions experienced in a timely manner. There may be instances where someone listened to you, but you didn't feel understood or empathetically heard, and that in itself may have added to your emotional burden. Determining the severity of the emotional harm and whether seeing a counselor or seeking additional methods of healing is necessary is a decision that only you can make.

Now, with all the insights you've gained, it's time to forgive, let go, and release. You are not meant to forget the experiences but to soften the pain to the point where it no longer controls you or occupies space in your present life. As you elevate your energy vibration, it's essential to detach from the past and attach to the present. When you let go of the past, you will watch your concerns diminish because the past is gone, the future hasn't arrived, and only the present is flowing in your life.

At this stage, you are ready to embrace the present and fulfill your life's purpose with happiness and peaceful mind, in alignment with divine destiny—exactly as you deserve.

Note: *The Libra Technique is named after the zodiac sign of Libra, which symbolizes justice and balance through its scales. This technique is grounded in the principles of fair* *self-assessment and introspection, aligning with the energies of Libra to promote personal evaluation and equilibrium. Additionally, Libra is my own birthdate zodiac sign, and this approach is a unique method designed by me to help individuals achieve a deeper understanding of themselves and their healing process.*

Etheric Cord Cutting Ritual

Everything in the world is based on energy. When you engage in emotional, verbal, or physical interactions with someone, an energetic connection, known as an etheric cord, is formed between you and that person. This invisible cord links your energy fields, and depending on the depth and nature of the relationship, it can be positive or negative, strong or weak. These energetic connections also exist between humans and animals or objects. However, in this context, we are focusing on human relationships.

Whenever you interact with someone, especially in a romantic sense, you create stronger cords. The intensity of these cords depends on the nature of the bond between the individuals. These invisible cords are reinforced through interactions, thoughts, and emotions. These connections allow you to both receive and send energy and, in some cases, even create telepathic communication.

The impact of these etheric cords is most profound in deep or intimate relationships. It is not uncommon to find that, even after years of ending a relationship with a friend or partner due to betrayal, lies, deceit, or harm, their image, thoughts, or memories still resurface in your mind. You might be wondering why this still happens, even after eliminating contact. The answer lies in the energetic cords that still need to be severed. Even without direct interaction, these cords may remain intact and drain your energy, leaving you emotionally depleted. That's why, even when your mind knows that walking away is the right choice, something deeper—often unconscious—can still create a lingering pull toward that person. Because of this connection, you may experience a strong sense that the other person is in danger or thinking about you. This form of telepathic communication is directly related to the presence of etheric cords.

In healthy relationships, these cords act as a source of positive energy, strengthening your being and fostering connection at the heart level. These energetic bonds can rejuvenate you, much like the uplifting energy felt after spending time with a loved one. However, in unhealthy relationships, these cords can become draining, pulling you into a state of emotional depletion. When a relationship begins to unbalance your energy field, signs such as feelings of attachment, anger, anxiety, resentment, fear, or obsession may arise. At this point, it's essential to use this technique.

The most effective way to prevent negative cords from forming is to avoid creating them in the first place. Maintaining a high vibrational frequency is the key here. The higher your vibration, the less likely it is for negative cords to develop. Additionally, practicing forgiveness and setting and maintaining healthy boundaries will help protect you from forming negative etheric connections.

Some relationships, such as those with immediate family members, may not allow for a complete physical disconnection. However, with this technique and by invoking your higher self and theirs during ritual, you can free yourself from the unhealthy, deeply ingrained spiritual connection. This allows you to release the energy drain caused by these ties, even if physical separation is not possible.

Negative cords typically form in two ways:

1. **Transformation of positive cords into negative ones:** A positive cord can gradually shift into a harmful one when the relationship no longer

serves your well-being, or when mutual care and respect are lost. This often happens when you, or the other person, no longer prioritize the other person's happiness.

2. **Pre-existing negative cords:** These cords are negative from the start. They often form when someone intentionally drains your energy, curses you, or attacks you mentally, emotionally, or spiritually.

How to Increase Your Energy Vibration

1. Practice Daily Gratitude

Gratitude instantly raises your frequency. Begin and end your day by listing three things you're grateful for. Feel it—not just think it.

2. Cleanse Your Body and Environment

Your physical state reflects your energetic state. Eat high-vibration foods (fruits, vegetables, water), reduce processed foods, and detox when needed. Also, cleanse your space by clearing clutter, opening windows, and using incense.

3. Connect to Nature

Spend time in nature. Walk barefoot on grass, sit under a tree, or listen to ocean waves. Nature restores energetic balance and grounds your spirit.

4. Use Sound Frequencies

Listen to music tuned to healing frequencies like 432 Hz or 528 Hz, use singing bowls, or chant sacred mantras like "OM." These vibrational tools align your energy field with harmony.

5. Meditate or Practice Breathing Exercises

Quiet the mind through meditation, even for ten minutes each day. Breathing exercises also calm the nervous system and increase your vibration instantly.

6. Surround Yourself with High-Vibe People

Energy is contagious. Choose to be around people who inspire, uplift, and support your growth. Release or set boundaries with those who consistently drain or manipulate your energy.

7. Affirm and Visualize

Use high-frequency affirmations like:
- "I am aligned with love and truth."
- "I am vibrating at the frequency of peace and abundance."

Visualize yourself surrounded by radiant light or living your ideal life as if it's already true while reciting affirmations.

8. Practice Yoga with Awareness

Yoga harmonizes the body, soul, and mind. It clears emotional blockages, strengthens your energy field, and centers you in the present moment. Even a short daily practice can uplift your entire state of being.

9. Dance Freely and Joyfully

Dance is a powerful and joyful release. Move your body intuitively to music that uplifts you. This natural form of self-expression moves stagnant energy and awakens your spirit.

Etheric Cord Cutting Steps

This technique is a metaphysical approach, complementing and stabilizing the Libra Technique, and its importance is indescribable. Perform it with full focus, belief, and sincere faith. Here's how you do it:

1. Find a Quiet Space

Sit in a comfortable position, such as a lotus or cross-legged position with your spine straight in a quiet and peaceful environment, free from distractions.

2. Breathe Deeply

Close your eyes and take several deep breaths, exhaling slowly and fully, longer than you inhale, while focusing completely on the movement of your belly. Allow your breath to become steady and calm.

3. Meditate

Spend a few minutes meditating while focusing on the present moment without judgment. You can do this in silence or while listening to calming meditation music or sounds of nature if you prefer.

4. Call on Your Spiritual Guides

Invoke the assistance of your spiritual guides and guardian angels to support you during this important process.

"Dear Spiritual Guide, I call upon your presence and guidance. Please assist me in healing and releasing any etheric cords that no longer serve my highest purpose. I ask that any cords connecting me to others that are not aligned with love, light, and positive attention be severed. Surround me with healing light to protect me from forming new negative connections. Thank you."

5. Visualize the Person and the Cord

Imagine the person you wish to cut the cords from standing or sitting in front of you. Feel the strength of the cord connecting you to them and how it drains your energy. Do not judge the person, just feel how they affect your energy field and make you feel. Picture the cord or rope that links you to this person, feeling its weight and influence.

6. Forgive and Let Go

Smile and call upon their higher self by name. Say: "I forgive you, and you forgive me. We tried this relationship, but it no longer serves us. You owe me nothing, and I owe you nothing. Let's separate our paths and begin a new, independent journey."

7. Cut the Cord

Visualize yourself holding a pair of scissors and confidently cutting the cord. As you do, say goodbye with contentment, a sense of peace and smile. It's helpful to have an actual string and scissors with you while visualizing. Once you've symbolically cut the cord, dispose of the string somewhere far from your home, or safely burn it to further signify the release.

8. Continue Meditating

Shift your focus to the abundant opportunities that surround you. Visualize yourself as free and liberated, like a bird soaring in the sky or a fish swimming freely in a river. Feel the sense of independence, knowing you need nothing and no one besides divine guidance and strength.

9. Visualize Protection

Imagine your energy field surrounded by a bright, shining golden-white light. This divine light forms a protective shield, safeguarding you from any negative energies, influences, or attachments, ensuring your peace and well-being.

10. Gratitude

With a deep sense of gratitude for the successful completion of this process, take three slow, deep breaths. As you exhale, feel a sense of closure and peace. Gently open your eyes, knowing you are free and protected.

11. Post-Session Cleansing

After completing the session, it's important to cleanse your energy. Drink plenty of fluoride-free water to help flush out any remaining negative energy. You can take a salt bath if you have a bathtub, or if not, soak your feet in a solution of pink Himalayan salt and water for up to ten minutes. For added cleansing, sprinkle a small amount of salt over your head, focusing on the crown chakra.

Final Notes

If the relationship you wish to disconnect from emotionally and energetically is very strong, such as with a spouse or ex-partner, it is recommended to perform this ritual for twenty-one consecutive days to ensure a thorough and lasting release.

If you are applying all three techniques of this book simultaneously, one deep meditation session with strong focus for an extended duration along with powerful visualization will be sufficient to achieve the desired results in partnership with other methods.

The meditation process should last at least twenty to thirty minutes. If you don't dedicate sufficient time to this process, don't expect significant results. The universe generously rewards your efforts, often surprising you with its abundance.

Note: *When you cut off the etheric cords that no longer serve you, the other person usually feels it. Although they may not understand the source or cause of this feeling, they might feel an unexplained void in your energy and feel inclined to reach out to you. This can be a temptation to fall back into the negative energy exchange, especially if the person is a romantic partner to whom you are still energetically attracted but who no longer serves you. If necessary, repeat the meditation until you feel their cords have been fully released.*

Full Moon Forgiveness Ritual

After completing the Libra Technique and the Etheric Cord Cutting Ritual, the next step is to harness the powerful energy of the full Moon, which enhances and complements the previous practices. The new Moon is the best time for setting the intention, while the full Moon is the best time to let go.

If you are unfamiliar with the full Moon's influence, consider how it affects the tides of the ocean. The Moon has a profound impact on the ocean's rhythm, yet we often fail to notice how it influences our own personal lives. This can symbolize the deep, hidden connection between humans and cosmic energies, which most people are unaware of. As we go about our busy lives, distracted by daily challenges and concerns, we become less aware of these energies and their influences.

The full Moon marks the peak of the lunar cycle, a time when energy is at its highest. During this period, emotions can be amplified, which is why some people may seem agitated or unsettled. The full Moon is a time of culmination—an opportunity to release old patterns, toxic habits, and unresolved emotions. It is a powerful time to let go of anything that no longer serves you: guilt, fear, anger, jealousy, bad habits, or any other negative energy that has accumulated in your life. The full Moon offers a chance for purification and healing, making it the perfect time for deep inner work.

Forgiveness is a key practice when it comes to releasing negative energy. To manifest your desires during the new Moon, it is essential to first let go of any grudges or emotional wounds you may carry. The full Moon is an ideal time to focus on forgiveness—both toward others and yourself.

Here's the metaphysical perspective that might make forgiveness easier: Before you were born, you likely made spiritual agreements with other souls. These agreements were designed to help your soul grow and evolve. The people who challenge you, hurt you, or trigger your deepest emotions are often fulfilling their role in these agreements without even knowing or remembering. They are, in essence, your teachers. Look for the lesson discomfort is teaching you. If you learn the lesson, you'll be able to move on. Ultimately, if you accept that you came to this planet to evolve, so that you no longer need to reincarnate, then perhaps you will make a greater effort to deal with your problems. That friend who truly bothers you is actually your teacher. That stranger who disrespects you is also your teacher. The teacher at school who treated you badly and upset you, your loved one, and even your own children are all your teachers.

Sometimes, you may forgive but not forget. And that's okay. While forgiveness is a powerful act, forgetting isn't always feasible. Forgiving someone doesn't mean what they did was right; it means you've made peace with it and are now ready to move forward.

When you hold onto anger, bitterness, or any negative emotion, you block the path to clarity and proper action. The emotions you carry shape the signals you send out into the universe, and these signals strongly influence how your life unfolds. According to the universal Law of Attraction, positive or negative thoughts bring corresponding positive or negative experiences into one's life—like attracts like, anger attracts anger, and hate attracts hate. When you hold onto anger, you're sending out negative energy. But when you forgive, you shift your energy, sending out purer, happier signals. By doing so, you make it easier to manifest your dreams and create the life you truly desire.

Every month during the full Moon, take a moment to forgive those who have hurt you, even if they may not be aware of the role they played in your life. Holding grudges only leads to bitterness, and this poison can block your spiritual growth. The full Moon doesn't always occur at night. It may happen anytime during the day. The best time to perform the Full Moon Forgiveness Ritual is the night before it happens, not the night after.

Full Moon Forgiveness Ritual

1. Acknowledge Your Feelings

Begin by giving value and worth to your emotions, including your anger or sadness. Stand in front of the mirror and repeat the following affirmation: "I have the right to feel upset about these events. I am valuable and deserve the best. Happiness and sorrow, forgiveness and anger are all part of the human experience. I am not alone." Reflect on the times you experienced anger and sadness, and consider how you navigated through them, ultimately growing from the experience. With time, you may come to recognize the wisdom these emotions have brought to your life.

2. Sit in Silence and Meditate

On the night of the full Moon, take a few moments to sit in silence and meditate. Use this time to forgive anyone you hold grudges against or feel resentment toward. If someone has hurt or upset you, ask their higher self for forgiveness for your negative feelings, and send them love. In turn, forgive them and release any lingering negativity. Allow this practice to bring peace and healing to you and those around you.

3. Take Deep Cleansing Breaths

Take a few slow, deep breaths to cleanse your mind and body.

As you inhale, imagine a bright white healing light from the galaxy streaming down through your crown chakra on top of your head and filling your body with peace and warmth, especially in your mind, throat chakra, and heart chakra. With each exhale, visualize black energy—stress, anger, hate, discomfort, events and people related to them—leaving your body through your mouth. Allow each breath to bring you closer to calm, clarity, and healing.

4. Create a List of Forgiveness

Think of anyone who has caused you pain or upset you, including individuals from your past, even from your childhood, whom you haven't forgiven yet. Write their names and describe the actions they took that hurt you. Allow yourself to write as much as needed. You have now created your list of forgiveness.

5. Visualize Each Person or Situation

Close your eyes and visualize each person, situation, place, behavior, or trauma one by one that has caused you distress. Picture them inside a pink bubble in your mind as pink represents love. Imagine them smiling at you, radiating goodwill. As you do this, say aloud several times, "I forgive you because I deserve peace." Finally, allow each person, situation, or memory to gently float away in their bubbles, releasing their holds on you.

6. Repeat the Full Moon Forgiveness Affirmation

Repeat the following affirmations aloud, sincerely and wholeheartedly, for your own well-being: "Under the glorious full Moon, I forgive everything, everyone, every experience, and every reminder from the past or present that requires forgiveness. I forgive all things with a positive heart. I also forgive myself for past mistakes. The universe is loving, and I am only under the rule of love. Love governs my life, and love flows freely. With this understanding, I am at complete peace."

You may also add: "I bring love and healing to all my thoughts, beliefs, and relationships. I learn my lessons and move forward. From the full Moon, I ask to cleanse the pieces of my soul and return them to me. I send love to myself, to everyone I know, and to everyone who knows me, across all directions of time. On this glorious full Moon, I heal. My life heals."

7. Burn Your Forgiveness List

Find a safe place, such as near a sink or another area where fire won't pose a danger. Use any natural flame to burn your forgiveness list. As you do so, feel the weight of the past lifting off your shoulders. Let the flames purify your emotions, releasing the grudges, pain, and attachments you've carried. At this stage, you can also burn the list created in Libra Technique, allowing both to be cleansed and released into the universe. Watch the flames transform your emotional burden into peace and freedom.

8. Embrace the Divine

Surrender to the loving embrace of the divine. Close your eyes, take a deep breath, see yourself free and light in a circular golden energy field, and feel the unconditional love and safety surrounding you. Allow yourself to be fully immersed in this divine protection and comfort, knowing that you are guided, loved, and supported on your journey of healing.

While performing the above ritual and writing your forgiveness list, you release resentment, creating space for something powerful to take its place. Gratitude is the highest quality to replace resentment. By cultivating gratitude, you elevate your vibration, which in turn enhances your happiness and overall well-being. The higher and purer your vibration, the more aligned and prepared you will be to manifest your desires during the new Moon. Gratitude helps shift you beyond the limitations of the ego, allowing you to attract your dreams with greater ease and clarity and to manifest whatever you want.

PART FIVE

Closing Reflections

Afterword

You've made it to the end—but in fact, this is only the beginning. Even still, congratulations on making it this far. It takes great courage to confront the truth, acknowledge your role in the past, and revisit painful memories. Many shy away from this work, but you have chosen to face it head-on. And that alone sets you apart from the majority. You should be proud.

This book was never just about healing the past but about remembering who you truly are beneath the pain, confusion, and conditioning. You've taken significant steps—facing your shadows, honoring your emotions, and learning the spiritual truths that govern your life. Having successfully completed the three core techniques—healing trauma, releasing unhealthy energetic attachments, and forgiving—you are now at a pivotal moment. It's time to place a stronger emphasis on self-awareness, spiritual growth, personal independence, and consciousness. This will ensure you do not repeat past patterns or fall into similar harms in the future.

In the past, you understood lessons in life with the level of awareness and knowledge you had at the time. But now, with your elevated soul and deeper understanding, boundless opportunities and achievements await you. You are no longer the same version of yourself who began this book. With each page, you've released old burdens, untangled karmic threads, and reconnected with your soul's purpose. You've learned that forgiveness is not a weakness but a powerful key to inner freedom. You now carry tools that many go their whole lives without discovering.

Even still, you must remember: Healing is not a one-time event. It is a conscious way of being. True healing of the soul begins with acceptance. When you acknowledge your role, peace and contentment follow naturally, creating space for healing to emerge. Throughout this journey, you've also gained deeper insight into the concepts of spiritual contracts and karma.

As you move forward, continue to practice the rituals, trust divine timing, listen to your intuition, and keep your energy field clear and positive. Let your life reflect your growth. Let your boundaries be sacred. Let your peace be non-negotiable. And above all, stay awake. Stay awake to who you are, to what you deserve, and to what no longer belongs in your life. The more you walk in alignment, the more life will meet you with grace, clarity, and purpose.

Most importantly, a healthy society is built on individuals who are mentally, emotionally, and spiritually balanced. Healthy individuals raise healthy children, and when society is filled with individuals who are conscious and harmonious, they collectively contribute to the greater good, walking the path of light and wisdom. It is my hope that this vision becomes a reality.

When the mind is free from the noise of overthinking, and rooted in presence, forgiveness and awareness, your thought waves begin to travel effortlessly into universe. In that quiet space, a deeper connection, where the universe can finally hear you, respond to you, and align with you, is formed. Living among higher frequencies allows you to attract experiences, people, and outcomes that match your true self. On the other hand, low vibrations only echo more of the same: confusions, fear, disconnection, negative people, and traumatic events. Real power lies not just in manifesting what you desire but in becoming a clear antenna—one that can receive, transmit, and tune into the vast intelligence of the universe. When you align with this frequency, the Law of Attraction is no longer a concept but a lived reality.

So, stay present, stay open, and stay tuned in. Because everything you are looking for is already looking for you.

Author's Word

Thank you for allowing me to be part of your healing journey. Though we may never meet in person, our souls have shared space in this sacred work. You are not alone, and you never have been. May you walk forward with a clear heart, a free soul, and a quiet mind. You are worthy. You are powerful. You are home. May this be your new beginning.

With deep love and gratitude,

Matin Ahaki Lakeh

Glossary

Energy

The life force that flows through all living things. Everything in the universe is made of energy, including your thoughts, emotions, and physical body. Energy can be high or low, blocked or flowing, and it greatly impacts your emotional, physical, and spiritual well-being.

Chakra

Chakras are spinning energy centers located along the spine, each corresponding to different physical, emotional, and spiritual aspects of your being. There are seven main chakras, and when they are balanced, your energy flows freely, and your overall well-being improves.

Higher Self

The Higher Self refers to the wise, eternal part of you that exists beyond ego and fear. Your Higher Self is connected to divine wisdom and always guides you toward your soul's purpose and inner truth. A person's Higher Self is the soul mind which is always functioning to prevent their human self from taking the wrong path.

Subconscious Mind

This is the part of your mind that stores beliefs, memories, and emotional patterns—many of which you are not consciously aware of. It influences your thoughts, behaviors, and reactions. Healing often involves working with the subconscious to shift deep-rooted patterns. The subconscious mind can also be defined as your soul mind which always exists, even when the logical and physical mind fade after death.

Law of Attraction

The Law of Attraction is a universal law stating that like attracts like. Your thoughts, emotions, and beliefs send out energetic signals that draw similar experiences back to you. What you focus on—positively or negatively—expands.

Law of Vibration

The Law of Vibration is the foundational principle that everything in the universe is in constant motion and has a vibrational frequency. Higher vibrations (love, joy, peace) attract similar energies, while lower vibrations (fear, anger, guilt) do the same. Raising your vibration helps you align with more positive outcomes.

Law of Cause and Effect

Also known as the Law of Karma, this universal principle states that every action—whether physical, emotional, or energetic—creates a corresponding reaction. Nothing happens by chance, and every experience is a result of previous causes, whether from this life or past lifetimes. This law teaches personal responsibility and helps us understand that we are co-creators of our reality through our thoughts, choices, and behaviors.

Ego

In spiritual terms, the ego is the false self—the part of our identity shaped by fear, separation, comparison, and attachment to the material world. It thrives on control, validation, and external achievement. While the ego serves a purpose in navigating physical reality, it can, when unchecked, block spiritual growth and keep us disconnected from our Higher Self. True healing often involves transcending the ego to reconnect with the soul's wisdom.

Acknowledgments

My deepest love and gratitude go to my beloved husband. His unwavering support and belief in my vision have been the foundation of this work. Through every stage of this process—doubt, inspiration, long nights, and quiet breakthroughs—he stood by me with patience, encouragement, and unshakable faith.

Without his love, presence, partnership, and encouragement, this book would not exist as it does today. For all the seen and unseen ways he has contributed to this creation, I am forever thankful.

About the Author

Matin Ahaki Lake, a spiritual and metaphysical practitioner, has always been a seeker drawn to the deeper truths of existence and guided by a quiet inner knowing that life is far more than what we see. From a young age, she experienced vivid moments of intuition and insight—subtle encounters with the unseen that couldn't be explained by logic alone. Those early moments of awareness opened the door to a lifelong exploration of unseen dimensions of energy, consciousness, and healing.

Over the years, her path has been shaped by personal experience, dedicated practice, and ongoing study across spiritual traditions and metaphysical teachings. While she embraces the role of a practitioner, she also considers herself a lifelong student committed to continued growth, refinement, and inner alignment.

This book, her first published work, is the result of many years of spiritual exploration, real-world application, deep introspection, and heartfelt research. It was written in her own time, with no outside pressure, born simply from a sincere desire to share what has helped her with those who may be searching for clarity, healing, or direction in their own lives.

Matin writes not from a place of perfection but from lived experience as someone who has walked through the shadows and returned with light. She offers this work as a guide to help others reconnect with their truth, heal from the past, and return to themselves. Her message is simple yet powerful: transformation is possible when the soul is ready, and the path, no matter how difficult, always holds meaning.

I would love to hear from you!

Contact me at

WisdomAscendant@gmail.com